Smoothie Power!

Recipes for

Weight Loss, Vitality,

&

the Occasional

Superpower

Smoothie Power!
Recipes for Weight Loss, Vitality,
& the Occasional Superpower

Copyright © 2012 by Diane Kidman

Printed in the United States of America
ISBN: 978-0-9839155-8-4

Cover Design by: Diane Kidman

Published by: carp(e) libris press, LLC

Visit the Author Website at:
www.DianeKidman.com

Table of Contents

Introduction – The Experiment

"So, what's the next book going to be about?"

"I don't know," I said. I was walking down a woodland trail with my husband, our son pumping away on his bike ahead of us. "I wanted to do something a bit less complex in the research department this time. Something I know so well it'll just flow."

"You should do a recipe book. It wouldn't be complicated if you base it off all the stuff you make, anyway," he said.

"Yeah, a recipe book! Easy peasy, lemon squeezy."

"Easy what?"

"Should I do soups? How about soups?" I was getting

excited.

"Nah, all your soup recipes are pretty much the same."

"Hey!" Defensive wife stride kicks in.

"How about your really great, fantastic, delicious smoothies?" Nice save, buster.

"Oh, smoothies. Good idea. I even have a bunch written in a tablet already. Maybe 20 or 30. Maybe 50, even." More accurately, about 5.

"Easy peasy!"

"Lemon squeezy?"

You have just enjoyed a reenactment of this book's conception stage. You may now uncover your eyes.

Once I settled on doing a smoothie book, my idea was to compile my family's favorite green smoothie recipes and create some exciting new ones, then pull them all together in an entertaining and easy-to-follow recipe book so others could enjoy them. Quick. Simple. Done lickety-split. I should know by now that never happens. The journey behind the writing of this book turned out to impact me personally, and in a big way. Something I never anticipated. Over the several months I spent testing and creating the recipes, I noticed surprising and unexpected changes in my own health. While I didn't intend to change my eating habits, I found that shortly after beginning the research for *Smoothie Power!* I lost my desire for sweets and gained strong cravings for fresh fruits and vegetables. I didn't feel the urge to snack on unhealthy foods anymore. My asthma began to lessen noticeably by the day, my lungs opening up like I never knew possible, until a lifetime of asthma seemed to dissolve. I lost nine pounds (three of it in one day). My skin got clearer and much softer, my vision improved, even scars I've had since childhood either faded or disappeared entirely. And my mental and physical energy skyrocketed. Kinda like Superman leaping a tall building. Or at least just me leaping a laundry basket without falling on my head.

Funny thing is, I'd already been drinking green smoothies for years. I discovered them while researching health right about the time my son was born. Since I myself was born a human and not a rabbit, chewing away at big piles of salad held little appeal. But drinking them? I could do that. I started throwing all manner of greens and fruit into a blender. Six months after giving birth, I lost all the baby weight and then some. I actually weighed less than I did before getting pregnant, and I kept that weight off.

Combining the green smoothies with a desire to eat healthier while nursing my baby, I shed my baby weight without thinking much about it. As the years went by, I continued to drink green smoothies sometimes once a week, other times daily, but I let go of the habit of drinking them regularly until researching for this book. Now that I've done it again and this time in larger quantities, I witnessed firsthand the power of adding a more dense form of super nutrients from raw fresh fruits and greens to my diet. I feel more prepared than ever to present to you these incredibly healthy smoothie recipes. I may even bend some steel in my bare hands just to prove it.

Answers to Your Smoothie Questions

I bet you have plenty of questions about green smoothies. Why are they so healthy? What do you need to get going? Will your IQ be raised 20 points and will you receive a raise for your on-the-job brilliance and acumen? Here's where you get the answers to some of your burning questions, or at least the stuff I wondered about when I first started drinking green smoothies. I'll also help you avoid some of the pitfalls I encountered, like chunky smoothies. Because chunky smoothies are just gross.

Who are Smoothies For?

Saying smoothies are for everyone sounds a little hokey perhaps, but they are. It's a safe addition to a healthy weight loss program without sending one into the tailspin of food denial that makes most diets fail in the end. Children benefit by being able to consume a healthy dose of all those fresh, leafy greens they'd never eat off their dinner plate, even if we begged a whole bunch with tears in our eyes. And for those with special dietary needs or health issues, it can be nothing short of a miracle. Diabetics have been able to reduce their insulin or even eliminate it, all while enjoying the deceptively sweet taste of a smoothie.

If you have allergies, asthma, diabetes, cardiovascular disease, arthritis, dermatitis, eczema, or other health issues that you thought could only be cured by handfuls of pills, your body may be trying to tell you that what you really need is nutrition. Yes, you still need to talk to your doctor about it if you have serious health concerns, but once you've got the green light, go for the green glass. We'll talk more about a few specific medical conditions in a moment.

Why Add Greens to your Smoothie?

Adding greens to your diet is vitally important for good health. They're loaded with phytochemicals and micronutrients and all the good, infinitesimally small but important things your body needs to work properly. Most of us, at least here in the U.S., don't consume enough greens, not by a long shot. I remember when I was growing up, one of the few greens you could find fresh at the store was iceberg lettuce. Sadly, this green contains practically nothing nutritional that our bodies crave. Yet, even now when a vast array of fresh greens are featured in most stores, iceberg tops the list as the most popular salad green. It's so inexpensive that it shows up on all the fast food burgers and burritos, giving consumers the wrong impression that they're getting a helping of vegetables with their burger. It offers a sprinkle of crunch if you're lucky, but not much beyond that.

Dark green leaves are the stuff you want. Are you afraid to throw it in your blender with (gasp!) fruit? Well, don't be. The wide array of recipes contained herein give you a good selection of smoothies without tasting like you're drinking lawn clippings. Instead, the fruit balances out the greens in such a way that you'll hardly know they're there. Unless you look at it. The green smoothies are green, after all.

Go Organic or Don't Bother?

If the whole "organic or not" question has you pacing the

produce aisles, you're not alone. Being health conscious is enough to keep some people up at night wondering if that standard, non-organic banana is doing them any harm when they're not looking. While there are some fruits and vegetables that are definitely best as organic, sometimes it's alright if you can't afford a $3 organic avocado. I'd rather you get a regular avocado than not eat any at all because you're afraid of its contents. That being said, it is best to get thin-skinned fruits and vegetables from the organic section of the produce department whenever possible, as thin skins mean more pesticides have found their way into the fruit. Apples, pears, plums, peaches, etc., do absorb more pesticides when they're sprayed. Bananas are thick skinned, but the pesticides used on them are pretty atrocious and are best avoided, if only for ecological reasons.

Here's a list of items best purchased as organic:

Apples

Bell Peppers

Blueberries

Celery

Cherries

Cucumbers

Grapes

Honeydew

Lemons

Lettuces and Greens

Nectarines

Oranges

Peaches

Pears

Plums

Raspberries

Tangerines

Tomatoes

Strawberries

Here are some items that are generally low in pesticides
if not purchased as organic:

Avocado

Cantaloupe

Grapefruit

Pineapple

Kiwi

Mango

Papaya

Watermelon

The bottom line is this: If you can afford organic, do. Get
all you can. Multiple studies worldwide show organic
produce contains a much higher concentration of
vitamins and minerals than their conventional

counterparts. But if you can't afford the higher prices of organic, don't avoid the fruits and vegetables altogether. It's better to eat them and learn to wash them very well than to lack those precious foods in your diet. Simply adding sufficient nutrition to your body will go a long way in combating any negative side effects from those non-organic items.

Whether you choose organic or not, make sure all your produce is ripe before you eat it. No green bananas or hard peaches in your smoothies. Those are difficult to digest and are green for a reason: They don't have everything ready for you yet.

How to Wash Non-Organic Produce

The process is simple. You can soak your items in a large bowl of water with a splash of white vinegar or a tablespoon of baking soda. Rinse thoroughly after that.

Soft items like apricots and peaches should not be soaked, but you can make your own fruit and vegetable spray with items you probably already have in your home.

Produce Spray

1 Tbs. lemon juice (Fresh, not the kind in the plastic lemon. That usually contains additives.)
1 Tbs. white vinegar
1 cup water
A new clean spray bottle

Spray your fruits and vegetables, then let them sit for five or 10 minutes before rinsing thoroughly.

For the organic fruits, veggies, and greens, you can choose to wash them or leave them as they are, au naturale. I'm still a washer when it comes to my organic produce because I can't help but think of all the possible scenarios the produce may have gone through before landing in my home, but some experts say we're better off when we consume some of that fresh, organic dirt along with our salad. A little grit adds microorganisms we need for healthy bodies. And the occasional little bug is good, too. (You don't really have to eat the bugs. I'm just saying.)

The Fresh or Frozen Question

Wondering if that bag of frozen strawberries is as good as fresh? If you're talking about comparing them to the basket you just picked up at the farmer's market, then probably not. But if it's mid-winter and there's not a fresh strawberry insight, aside from the stuff shipped from the other side of the equator, you'd best grab the frozen bag.

Frozen fruits are picked at their peak of ripeness, then immediately washed and frozen. That means off season it's the closest you'll get to fresh. While the blanching process required to kill off bacteria before freezing also kills off vitamin A along with the B vitamin called thiamine, the rest of the nutrients are pretty much intact. In fact, a 2003 Austrian study discovered that there's more nutrition in seasonally frozen produce than there is in out-of-season imported produce.

Why? Because in order for that imported strawberry to get to you before it starts to turn into a fuzzy little mush pile, it must be picked well before it's ripe. Therefore, the strawberry does all its ripening on a big truck in the dark, without its cute little leaves and the roots and soil and sunshine. Not much happening on the vitamin and mineral front, is there?

Overall, it's best to eat seasonally and locally, but that's rather hard knocks for us in the northern climes. We're kind of short on local fresh fruit come December. So the overall answer? Eat fresh whenever it's in season; eat frozen whenever it's not.

How Many Greens Should One Consume?

It used to be that when I'd read various books on health and nutrition, I'd balk at their suggestions for fruit and vegetable intake. Three cups of this, five cups of that, six of this fruit, four of that vegetable - all in one day? It sounded ridiculous, and I couldn't imagine how anyone could eat like that. I envisioned myself seated at the dinner table, a large mixing bowl loaded with raw kale and spinach, three bananas at my side, and a pile of carrot sticks in the form of a small log cabin. I don't think I need to tell you how impossible this picture was to bear. It made my jaws ache.

But now that I drink green smoothies every day, three cups of spinach or kale seem like nothing to me. I put a good two packed cups of greens into every quart of smoothie I make, and I drink two or three quarts a day. And now that I just about crave salads by the truckload, it's easy for me to consume more greens than is even required. (Yes, it's alright to eat even more.)

So, how many greens should you have? If you're drinking green smoothies daily, try to incorporate three packed cups of dark leafy greens into your drinks throughout the day. When they're not in smoothies but perhaps in salads, five cups are best. Another reason blending your greens is a magnificent idea: You get more bang for your buck. Blending the greens breaks down and provides more nutrients to your system, and in a more direct and easily digestible form.

How Many Smoothies Should One Consume?

You can ultimately drink all the smoothie you want to, although I recommend you start off with a glass or two on the first day and build your way up. The interesting part about smoothies is that since they contain the whole fruit and leaf, they're much more filling than you'd imagine. You might think you'll be able to put away gallons of the stuff, but you won't. For instance, I usually make a quart of smoothie in the morning for myself. It takes maybe an hour for me to work my way through it, and after that, I'm simply not hungry for anything else. It's breakfast. That may seem odd, but set the ingredients out for one smoothie and envision it as your breakfast. The smoothie is especially beneficial for people like me who tend to shun breakfast anyway, no matter how many times we hear it's the most important meal of the day. Finally, a comfortably full stomach in the morning.

The stomach is designed not just to measure the amount of food you put in it, but the amount of nutrients. If you fill it with foods lacking in nutrients, it eventually gets full (and uncomfortably so) by sheer volume, but it won't take long before your stomach is crying for more. "Okay, enough with the cheeseburger," it'll tell you. "Where are my nutrients? Send more down!" And so many of us do, trying to trigger that full meter but never actually hitting it. We eat more and snack more and get hungry again and... I'll bet this sounds familiar to all of us. But what the stomach wants are the nutrients. Not just the bread and chips and grease. Oh, and that's another thing: Oils, especially trans fats, require us to eat much, much more to get that "full" meter registering. Once your body is turned onto all the goodness in the green smoothies, you'll be surprised at how fast you start filling up!

Smoothies on a Budget

Most of us don't have a bottomless wallet from which to purchase whatever groceries our hearts desire. And sadly, one of the biggest reasons many people refrain from adding more fresh produce to their diet is the misconception that it will cost them more. Yes, a big container of organic mixed baby greens can look awfully excessive in price when seated next to a head of iceberg lettuce, but remember that with your newfound diet, that box of greens will be the basis of several meals, hence replacing other more pricey items you might normally purchase from the processed food aisle.

During my first trip to the store before preparing smoothie recipes for this book, I loaded up the cart with a large variety of greens and fruit. My husband and I had a blast flinging things into our cart. "What's this? Cactus leaves? Get three." I bought fruits and greens I never had before, and when we looked in that full shopping cart, all I could think of was the price tag. Let me tell you this: Greens take up a lot more room in your shopping bags than meat, canned goods, and boxed meals. They're also cheaper. I can get a 3-pound container of organic spinach at my local Costco for around four dollars, and from that I can get about four or five quarts of smoothie when I add some fruit and water. I can't get a tray of meat for the same price that will become three or four meals. Therefore, I didn't suffer the sticker shock at the checkout that I'd expected.

Also remember that when you add green smoothies to your diet, you'll become less likely to purchase the extra junk food items such as cookies and chips. Those things add up fast to both your wallet and your waistline.

But where will you experience the biggest savings of all? Doctor visits, surgeries, medications, consultations, specialists, and other needless medical expenses we often get saddled with as a result of an unhealthy diet. Eliminating medical expenses, not to mention eliminating the mental and emotional stresses related to living with poor health, are truly priceless.

Oxalic Acid Myth Buster - Is it Dangerous?

I'm about to go out on a limb here. If you've ever heard talk of oxalic acid occurring in things like dark leafy greens, namely spinach and collards, you might have heard it said that it's a dangerous substance that will block your calcium absorption and make you ill. Some people are so cautious of oxalic acid they shun uncooked greens and even completely avoid spinach for reasons other than thinking it's yucky. But is it true? Can it make you sick?

Here's where I climb the tree and creek out onto that

limb. I'm going to say "no" to that, or at least "very rarely." I researched this question until my eyes crossed, and I was not able to find any legitimate proof to suggest that eating too many raw greens would make you sick. I dug through medical journals and research papers. I scanned the Internet to see what the pros had to say. I checked my favorite sources and read what the most trusted experts suggested. I went through numerous books on health, vegetarianism, and raw food veganism. What I found was precious little information on the subject and no solid discussions on whether or not we should worry about oxalic acid. In fact, the only places I found lots of heated discussion were online forums and blog comments wherein theories and scary stories about peoples' second cousins' neighbors' Uncle Bob died after sitting too close to a patch of spinach, etc.

In case you're still in the dark about oxalic acid, it's an organic compound present in many leafy greens, vegetables, and wild edibles. It's what people are talking about when they tell you not to eat uncooked rhubarb leaves (which you still shouldn't do, as they do contain a very high level of oxalates). Sure, it's an occasional cause for concern if you're a cattle rancher. (I mean the kind of cattle rancher whose cows still eat grass.) On rare occasion, cattle and other grazing animals suffer from oxalic acid poisoning when they have a limited variety of grasses to munch. This could be the very reason this compound exists - to keep grazers from eating away an entire species of plant. But can it get you?

I found no solid evidence that could happen, aside from a possible cause for concern in those prone to kidney stones. I would, however, recommend rotating your greens, if for no other reason than to assure you get the widest array of nutrients in your diet possible. And I've no doubt eating a whole bunch of the exact same greens day after day after day would have some negative effects, other than just extreme boredom of palate. After all, balance is key in all aspects of life. So make sure to get a wide variety of all fresh fruits and vegetables, and you won't have to worry about the oxalate question.

If you are prone to kidney stones or if your doctor has advised you against eating foods containing high levels of oxalates, then please do talk to your doctor before consuming large quantities of greens such as spinach, kale, dandelion, and Swiss chard. Otherwise, I'd say keep a balanced diet and let the blog forums worry about the dangers of a healthy diet.

Specific Health Concerns

Before we dive into the how-to's and then finally the recipes, it's important to take a moment and discuss any specific health concerns you may have. If you're a diabetic hoping to ditch your insulin, are pregnant and wanting to give that baby an excellent head start in life, or are the proud owner of a shih tzu with a pudgy waistline, here's where we touch on special considerations. This should set your mind at ease. (Yes, even you with the shih tzu.)

Detoxing

It's true - there can be side effects when you first start consuming lots of green smoothie. Your body may have some serious healing to do, and if that's the case, you're about to give it all the nutrition it needs to make that healing possible. Even if you consider yourself to be a very healthy individual already, you probably still have something or other that needs tuning up. No one was more surprised than I when I first began experimenting with smoothie recipes. I started out drinking about two to three quarts of smoothie a day and didn't give it much thought. I was my own guinea pig, after all. I wanted to come up with as many delicious recipes as I could. Imagine my surprise when, within the first couple of days, I was already feeling much different. My asthmatic lungs were opening up, my vision seemed clearer, the whites of my eyes brighter.

While those are all fantastic side effects, I also didn't expect a bout of headaches, achy legs, and sudden feelings of fatigue after what seemed like a glorious two-week long burst of energy. What was happening? Detox, my friend.

For most of us, a lifetime of eating things we shouldn't,

taking prescription and perhaps even recreational drugs, smoking, inhaling pollution, and more atrocities, our bodies have a storehouse of toxins they don't quite have the resources to handle. If our nutrition isn't ideal, our bodies set a lot of those toxins aside to be dealt with on another day when we feed it what it needs to clean house. When we begin to feed it correctly, it will start pulling out the brooms and dustpans, kicking up a horrible mess. All those boxes of carcinogens kept in the back of the closet under our prom dresses start coming out and being dumped - right into our bloodstream.

Other possible side effects can be diarrhea and skin breakouts or rashes. Usually, any heavier discomfort will be over in a matter of days. Depending on how much is stored in your system, however, it could take the body up to a few years to dispose of it all, little by little. But don't worry. Even if you've got a lot of repairs to get done, you won't feel bad all that time. For most people it's a rough patch that goes away after a short period. For myself, I even noticed that while I was experiencing headaches and a sore throat, I still somehow felt better than I had in the past. The energy would burst on the scene, or I'd feel more at peace and be able to handle situations with calm instead of calamity. It was worth keeping on, no doubt about it.

I personally didn't notice detox sensations until about the two-week period, although the very first day I started drinking all those smoothies, I experienced an odd combination of fatigue and elation. Which was fine. I sat next to the kiddie pool and contemplated my navel, something we all should partake of every now and again.

About two weeks later when I did hit that detox wall, I was feeling it for about five to seven days; but everyone's different. Again, this is another good argument for why you should check with your doctor before undertaking a big change in diet. (Incidentally, most doctors won't be in on the whole smoothie thing, so be prepared to explain exactly what it is you intend to do. Arm yourself with the kind of information a doctor would like to know about a diet change. Any details you can provide will help him or her to have a more complete understanding, and hopefully to get on board and lend you their support.)

For Weight Loss

Need to lose a bit of weight? Need to lose a whole lot of weight? That first green smoothie puts you well on your way. There's nothing better for weight loss than giving your body a healthy helping of dense, green nutrition. And if you're thinking of green smoothies as a "diet plan," you can toss that tired old phrase right out the window. This isn't a diet plan, it's not a late-night infomercial spiel, and you don't have to pay through the nose for funny boxed dinners or suffer through serious food denial to do it. You just have to drink your smoothies.

By starting out each day drinking a quart of green smoothie, you've just given yourself a wonderful and filling breakfast. Carry the glass around with you. Take the smoothie to work in a thermos or drink it on the way to the office. Preparing them requires at most two minutes. Cleanup is very minimal because you don't have to scrub. (Look, Ma, no grease!) And even if you don't care for breakfast much, a smoothie is easy to digest. And it's filling. Did I mention it's filling?

If you're worried you'll want to splurge and eat a big breakfast anyway, drink the smoothie first. Then see how you feel. Most people are surprised at how satisfied and comfortably full they feel. Light, but not empty. Satiated.

You can use smoothies to replace lunch, too, if you're so

inclined. Or drink a second quart of smoothie (a different recipe, one that really appeals to you) about an hour before your usual lunchtime. Then if you're still hungry at lunch, try one of the raw soup recipes that come later in this book. Add in a big salad with some healthy salad dressing, also found later in the book. I bet you won't be able to finish it all.

Prepare yourself healthy snacks in case you get the munchies midday. A moderate handful of raw almonds, walnuts, sunflower seeds, or cashews is a great way to stave off hunger. Keep a big bowl of cut up veggies in the fridge, and include one of the healthy salad dressings as a dip. And don't forget eating an apple or a small bowl of grapes. These are all great and healthy options.

About an hour before dinner, you can have a third quart of smoothie if you like. Again, make sure to try a different recipe. Variation is key. Look for ingredients you crave so you're satisfying cravings while you enjoy the smoothies. You'll be surprised at your rapidly rising energy levels and your lack of interest in other foods.

If it does happen that you had smoothies and healthy food all day long, then cracked at dinner when your husband decided to bring home a sack of burgers and fries, don't berate yourself. Don't get upset and think you've failed. Just pay special attention to how you feel after the burgers and fries, how different you feel than you do after consuming the green smoothies or raw soups. It's going to feel surprisingly different. Uncomfortable, even. Keep a journal and write down your observations. Turn what could have been viewed as a "failure" into a "test."

Also keep track of all your progress. Weigh yourself each morning before eating anything, and weigh yourself at the same time each day. If the weight remains the same for awhile, that's okay. There will probably be plateaus. If it bounces up a bit, take a look at what you're eating besides the smoothies and make adjustments to the kinds of fruits you're using in the smoothies. Are there lots of dates going in there? Too much honey or sweeteners? Avocado? Try backing off of these fattier items until your weight is where you want it.

I mentioned at the beginning of this book that I lost nine pounds after starting on green smoothies, and it's true. While I understand nine pounds isn't a whole lot, it did happen in only one month, and when I wasn't attempting to lose any weight. I was just experimenting with recipes. Those who drink green smoothies for weight loss - even into the hundreds of pounds - encounter startling results when they stick to it. For starters, it's the opposite of traditional dieting because you're feeding yourself, not starving yourself. This isn't about denial. It's about satisfying yourself and having more energy.

And speaking of energy, you'll experience the big surprise of wanting to move more, wanting to exercise. A few weeks after I started on them, I kept thinking of running. A few months into it, I was having dreams about running. Not the "running away from bad guys" scenario, but running for the pure joy of it. Sometimes during the day, it felt as if I just had to move my arms and legs. I ran up and down the stairs with the laundry basket, trotted from one end of the house to the other, chased the dogs in the back yard just because. (They liked that.) Finally, I went out and bought running shoes. Me. The girl who used to only run when a stinging insect or an ironing board was present. Nothing makes adding exercise to your daily routine easier than actually having the energy to do it.

If you've got a substantial amount of weight to lose and

you're ready to add green smoothies to your day, let your doctor in on what you're going to be doing. If your doctor isn't on board with things like increasing nutrients to decrease weight, it's probably time you find a doctor who will work with you. They're out there, and having one on your side will be invaluable.

Want a bit more inspiration? Check out my website at www.DianeKidman.com. I've pulled together some of my favorite inspirational finds from all over YouTube: green smoothie testimonials on weight loss and other healthy changes brought on by increasing one's intake of whole, raw fruits, greens, and vegetables.

For Those on a Low Sugar Diet

If your doctor recommends a low sugar diet, you can still drink green smoothies with fruit. Try and steer clear of the sweeter fruits like bananas, and instead stick with berries and apples and other fruits that contain less sugar until your doctor gives you the good news your diabetes has gone missing, which has happened for countless people. This includes Sergei Boutenko, son of green smoothie revolutionary Victoria Boutenko. In his case, it was Type I diabetes, which is not an easy one to break and is usually considered a permanent condition. As it turns out, dark leafy greens help lower your blood sugar. Good news, indeed, for the diabetic.

If your smoothies don't seem very appealing to you at first, being not so very sweet, try stevia extract. The stevia plant has been used for centuries in South America, and since it's 300 times sweeter than sugar, a little goes a long way. A couple of drops of that in a tall glass of smoothie adds a lot of sweetness and is much more economical and natural than the little stevia packets, which usually contain additives. And since stevia won't affect your glucose levels (it's not a sugar), you get a safe dose of sweetness. This is the only natural sweetener I know of that has no effect on glucose levels.

For Those on Medication

Countless people have reported eliminating their prescription medications after adding regular green smoothie consumption to their diets. Many of the common ills and diseases present in Americans and a growing number of people worldwide are things that can be prevented or reversed with a nutrient rich diet, such as that gained from green smoothies. Does this mean you can click your heels three times and toss all the pills out the window after your first quart of green smoothie? Certainly not. As with anything in life, moderation is key.

So what do you do if you've got a medicine cabinet full of little brown bottles with your name on it? Monitor your health closely. (I'd recommend keeping a journal.) Continue taking your medication, tell your doctor you've changed your diet, have your doctor test you regularly. If you feel any differences in your health and think your medications are suddenly too strong, never, ever toss them out without consulting your doctor first. Many medications require a patient to taper off of them, in order to avoid unpleasant and even dangerous side effects. Extra care should always be taken whenever making changes to your diet and your medications.

For the Seriously Ill

In cases of serious disease or illness, I'm all for including green smoothies in the treatment - right after talking to your doctor. I'm risking sounding like a broken record in order to ensure your safety, what with all the advice on talking to your doctor. I realize your doctor may not be very focused on nutrition, and perhaps he's never even heard of a green smoothie. But he does understand your medications and your condition. If you feel like your doctor doesn't understand the importance of nutrition, or that he isn't taking the time to get to know your circumstances or work with you on trying a healthier approach, it's probably a good time to shop for a doctor who will. Having the right doctor by your side is invaluable during serious illness.

I think it's especially important for organic produce to come into play if you're seriously ill. With lowered resistance, you may not be able to tolerate pesticides and insecticides as well as if you were in full health. Remember, too, that organic produce contains much higher levels of vitamins and minerals, things you'll want plenty of if you're trying to combat something serious. However, if all you can afford is non-organic produce, then get it. Just be sure to wash it thoroughly as discussed in the previous section of this book.

If you have a loved one that is battling an illness or disease and you're contemplating running out to get a blender to make them smoothies, be careful. Not everyone will understand your enthusiasm. While I'd love to hear that you were able to make green smoothies for your bedridden mother until she was back on her feet and healthier than ever, please remember that she might not get why you want her to change her diet when the doctor assured her she was incurable, and that her current diet is just fine. In these instances, the best approach may be to change your own diet and lifestyle, allowing your loved one to witness the changes in you without any gloating or lecturing on your part. It's easier to change your mind when someone isn't doing the "I told you so" dance before you. We all like to keep our dignity intact. Besides, there's nothing like having someone insist we make a major lifestyle change to convince us to dig our heels in even further.

If you're the one battling the illness, use caution and learn to listen to your body. As you begin to increase the nutrients through drinking green smoothies, keep notes. As mentioned earlier, a journal is an excellent idea. It allows you to see your progress, learn ways to improve, and notice what it is you're doing right. Write down what you want to share with your doctor. The better you are able to keep track, the better information you'll have. Perhaps your changes will inspire your doctor and even help someone else!

Drinking Smoothies While Pregnant or Nursing

Becoming pregnant changed my whole view on how I fed myself. It wasn't just about taking care of me anymore, and I started to see the food I ate as something that actually entered my body and directly affected my health. More importantly, I realized it entered my baby's body and directly affected his health. If I had only known about green smoothies, I would have started drinking them way back then. As it is, I'm glad I discovered them while nursing, which meant I still had prime opportunity to pass all those nutrients on to my son. That's always made me feel pretty good.

If you're pregnant and wondering if smoothies are okay for you, the answer is a resounding yes. The healthy benefits available to you and your baby are exciting. You'll be able to maintain better energy throughout your pregnancy, and the nutrition you'll be receiving can help strengthen you and baby for a safer delivery. Your weight gain during pregnancy will have a better chance of being at a healthier and more stable rate, and returning to your before-baby weight will be easier. A better night's sleep is more possible when you're eating healthy, not just for you but for baby. (Unborn babies sure enjoy bouncing around at night, don't they?) And all that talk of folic acid? You'll be golden. Dark leafy greens are loaded with folic acid. For instance, one cup of spinach contains 263 mcg of folate, whereas oranges, the food everyone likes to credit as a great source, only contains 40 micrograms of folate. (Don't misunderstand me, eat your oranges because they're so good for you. But spinach, collards, and turnip greens are the real folic heroes.)

If you decide to drink green smoothies during pregnancy, there are a few things to watch out for. First and foremost, don't decide to drink them by the gallon in the hopes of producing a super baby. Balance is important. I think the best bit of advice is to drink them until you're full or don't want any more. You don't want to choke down something unappealing or force yourself to consume as much as possible. This is a matter of nourishing yourself and your baby. Learn to listen to your body. If you drink some until you feel satisfied, that's the best way to go about it for anyone, pregnant or not.

That's also true for nursing mothers. Drink what you feel comfortable drinking. You can certainly have a quart or two throughout the day, but don't ever force yourself to consume more than is comfortable. Your body tells you when you've had enough. It will also begin to tell you what you need, so if one fruit or green suddenly seems more appealing than what you usually prefer, go with it!

Another precaution to take: Go for the organic whenever possible. This is an important time to avoid pesticides, fungicides, and the like. Make sure to wash all produce thoroughly, and if it's a difficult item to wash, soak it very well as described previously, or avoid it for now and stick with fruits, greens, and vegetables you feel you can wash well.

Also, remember that if you suddenly start drinking lots

of green smoothies, you could send yourself into detox mode. That's great if you're not pregnant or nursing. Getting toxins out of the body is an excellent idea. But for the pregnant or breastfeeding mom, going through detoxification can be too hard on the baby, not to mention tapping into the energy you need right now. So take it easy, enjoy your smoothies, and if you feel any detoxing side effects such as headaches, fatigue, diarrhea, skin breakouts, or flu-type aches and pains in your joints and muscles, back off the smoothies a bit and see if that was the cause. I know, I know. The list of side effects I just gave you describes a lot of the things pregnant women face, anyway. But if you experience those after a smoothie and don't experience them when you haven't had any smoothie, then moderate your intake.

As always, let your doctor and/or midwife in on what you intend to do. She may have very good advice for you as to which fruits or greens might be best for you and your baby. The more informed you become and the more you listen to both your body and your doctor, the healthier you and your baby will be.

Kids and Smoothies

I mentioned that smoothies are great for just about everyone, and that definitely includes the kids. Children of any age can enjoy smoothies. My six-year-old certainly doesn't drink the two quarts a day that I do, but he does enjoy somewhere between one and two cups a day. He likes to get involved in deciding what should go into it, and I always tell him what greens he's drinking. He's been enjoying them since he was old enough to hold a cup, so there has never been a distrust of that green stuff in his glass. And because we make it a fun part of our everyday lives, it's never been viewed as odd or icky.

If you're trying to introduce green smoothies to resistant

children, try the sippy cup or water bottle trick, wherein they don't have to look at the color. Or give the drinks fun names like "Bug Punch" or "Princess Juice." Adding some fresh or frozen blueberries to the mix will change the color entirely, often offering up an attractive purple beverage that may seem more appealing. Also, try serving the smoothies up in fun glasses with straws, or add some fresh sliced fruits to the side of the glass. Sprinkle the top with a dash of cinnamon or nutmeg. If they're old enough, get them involved in preparing the fruit or hauling out the greens. Before you know it, they'll come running the instant they hear your blender whirring away. I just about trip over my own son every time I hit that "on" switch.

One of the best parts about giving children smoothies is watching their tastes for healthy foods improve over time. My son has never been very thrilled about eating fresh raw greens, such as in a salad. Most kids aren't too hip on lettuce or chewy leafy stuff. But after just a week of being my official kid taste tester, I found he was eating all the salad off his plate at dinner without me haranguing him, sometimes even asking for seconds! One afternoon when we were eating in our favorite vegetarian restaurant, I caught my son reaching over and sneaking all the fresh romaine lettuce off my plate. Of course I didn't stop him.

You'll probably also find that if your child hasn't been in the habit of eating too many fresh fruits, he or she might start asking for them. Once the body discovers it feels good after eating certain things, it does indeed start craving them, no matter the age.

As for quantity, it's good for kids to have a pint of green smoothie a day. If they'd like more, that's fine, too. Just like adults, they're often able to find the "full" level pretty easily when consuming truly healthy foods. Also, make sure to never force smoothies on your kids, no matter how bad you want them to enjoy the health benefits. It's better to find a combination of fruits and greens, funny little cups, and twirly straws that they truly enjoy and want, rather than accidentally teaching them that healthy eating involves gagging and icky flavors.

Pets and Smoothies

Yes, pets can have smoothies, too. While Fido doesn't need a bowlful of green goodness every day like you do, he will benefit greatly from a few tablespoons several times a week. Most dogs and cats will munch on the lawn or eat leaves when given the chance. If you were thinking Fido was sort of mental, he really isn't. He's just craving his greens. My two miniature dachshunds look forward to that special treat from the blender and even beg for it. Funny thing is, one of my dogs, Liesl, has always enjoyed chewing leaves and grass more than her brother, Ralph. She even keeps one area of our lawn freshly clipped at all times. (We don't treat our lawn, so she has lots of safe and somewhat weedy vegetation to choose from.) I thought for sure she'd be the dog to really dig into her smoothie, but surprise, surprise, it turned out to be our bug eater. I guess Ralph instinctively laps up his smoothie, while Liesl has sometimes already had enough greens for the day, thank you very much.

Cats enjoy smoothies too; however, they need a bit of an alteration to theirs. Cats have a hard time digesting fruits, so their smoothies should be simply greens and water. Again, just a couple of tablespoons at a time should suffice.

Overall, smoothies are an excellent idea for your beloved pets and will bring them a wealth of healthy benefits, especially if they typically eat dried commercial foods.

This pack of nutrition will help their skin, their coat, and every other area of their health.

Note: I'm sorry I have no information on feeding smoothies to animals such as hamsters or anacondas. I know you love them, too. I can say with a great deal of certainty, however, that smoothies and goldfish do not mix. (For that matter, neither do hamsters and anacondas.)

How to Make Green Smoothies

Here's where we learn what to put in your green smoothies, what one tool is needed to make them, and how to whip one up in no time. Don't worry, it's easy. In fact, your time in the kitchen is about to become much shorter. Aren't you glad?

Now, if only we could figure out how to make that work for ironing…

What to Put in a Smoothie

I've seen many smoothie recipes out there that incorporate nuts, seeds, vitamin supplements, even protein powder. But the best, healthiest smoothies are those that contain nothing more than fruits, greens, and water, according to green smoothie guru Victoria Boutenko. Ms. Boutenko should know; she's credited with having invented the green smoothie, and she's done extensive research on our bodies' ability to absorb the nutrients. Nuts, seeds, and other additives - even vegetables - can make the nutrients harder to digest, causing gas and bloating. So instead of adding carrots and celery to your drink, set these otherwise healthy items aside for later.

In this book, you'll notice most of the recipes contain only four ingredients: two kinds of fruit, one kind of green, and water. That's not to say you can't veer from this formula. I've done this specifically to keep the recipes easy. I also like the idea of having only a few items in the smoothie so as to get the most benefit from each. The more ingredients you add, the less benefit each individual fruit or green can provide you.

If I ask you, "What's a fruit?" you'd probably list off things like apples and bananas, peaches, maybe watermelon. But what else is a fruit? You can add cucumber, tomato, and avocado to the list. Basically, a fruit contains seeds. Vegetables are starchy and are often in the form of a root or tuber. But to spare you the confusion, just know that what are included in my recipes are indeed all fruits and greens, with the very rare exception of a celery stick.

Greens are - well, they're green. And they're leafy. Think kale, spinach, collard greens, chards, dandelion greens, even carrot greens, celery greens, and radish greens. The possibilities are endless, and when mixed with fruit, are not overwhelming in leaf flavor. While you will come to love that chlorophyll taste, even crave it, you won't have to put up with it until you've developed a taste for it. I think spinach is a great starter green. The flavor is very mild, so much so that a couple of fruits and some water later, you won't even know it's there aside from the color. (Incidentally, some folks can't stand the sight of green *anything* when it comes to their food, especially those tiny folks we call kids. In those instances, remember to put the smoothie in a nice cup or water bottle that can't be seen through. This is also excellent for smoothie enthusiasts who are sick of explaining to everyone at the office what that green stuff is sitting on their desk.)

Whenever you can, use the best purified water you can get for your smoothie. We've kept things clean so far with healthy ingredients, so keep the ball rolling with fresh, pure water. It's definitely worth the investment to install a water purifier at the kitchen sink.

Sweetening Your Smoothie

When you first start making smoothies, they might not seem very sweet to you. Back in the early days, my smoothies almost always contained orange juice instead of water! While the smoothie was still healthy, the amount of sugar in them from the juice couldn't have been. It's a big reason I limited my family's smoothie intake - I was afraid all that orange juice combined with bananas and other super sweet fruits was overdosing my family on sugar when what I really wanted was a healthy drink. When making the recipes for this book, I definitely opted for water, the way I believe it should be done. My first smoothie with water tasted good to me, but I missed the sweetness my taste buds were used to. I found a bottle of stevia extract in my cupboard which contained no funny additives and was simply stevia, water, and denatured alcohol. (Sorry to say, adding some to your smoothie won't create a tropical cocktail, however. Stevia is so hyper-sweet in taste that you'll need a mere one to three drops to sweeten a whole glass.)

I found that adding a drop or two of stevia extract to my son's smoothies made them much more palatable for him, too. He's tried almost every recipe in this book, and when he found one not so thrilling, I added the stevia. Most of the time it worked like magic. I love that I don't have to worry about his sugar intake when I add stevia, because stevia is *not* a sugar. With a glycemic index of less than one, it's a very good natural alternative when you go for real stevia. (The little packets of white stevia have been processed and may contain additives. I recommend the extract.)

Another way to keep things on the sweeter side is to add things such as banana or pitted dates. Banana works as a sort of emulsifier as well, adding a creamy, smooth texture. It's also easy on the blender if you don't have a high powered one yet. Dates, on the other hand, definitely add the sweetness, but they're more difficult to blend with low powered blenders. Even with a powerful blender, you may prefer to soak the dates in some warm water for a few minutes before adding them to the smoothies. (And always check for pits, even if your dates are pitted. I can't tell you how many times I've missed a pit and had to quick shut off the blender. It's the biggest reason I switched over to a pure date paste with no additives or preservatives.)

I sometimes like adding raw organic honey. While this natural sweetener still does raise glucose levels and is even 70% fructose, it's at least a healthier and unprocessed alternative with its own nutritive properties, making it a far better choice than - shall we say it? Artificial sweeteners. Never, ever use those.

I can't go without mentioning agave, and unfortunately, I won't be recommending this one. That's because agave syrup or nectar is heavily processed (even if it says "raw" on the bottle) and is as much as a whopping 97% fructose! Even high fructose corn syrup, which I think we all understand is very unhealthy, is a "mere" 55% fructose. That's saying quite a lot. For any health conscious individual, agave doesn't sound very appealing, does it?

No matter how you choose to naturally sweeten your smoothies, you won't have to be concerned about keeping them sweet for too long because an interesting thing is about to happen to your taste buds. You'll need less and less sugary sweetness the longer you drink the smoothies. In fact, smoothies you start out with may seem repulsively sweet after only a few weeks! If it takes you a few months or even a year, however, don't feel guilt ridden. Everyone's different, and the important thing is that you're getting all that wonderful nutrition into you. Your body will take care of the rest.

How Long a Smoothie Lasts

Smoothies are always best fresh, but they can handle limited storage. You can keep your smoothie concoctions in the refrigerator for up to three days if you don't ravenously drink them before that. I like to keep a large 2-quart Mason jar around so I can store any pre-made smoothie in a nice tightly sealed container. It's easy to see that way, and I don't forget it's there. And because the lid seals so nice and tight, I can give it a good shake before serving it.

If you're traveling or need to take your smoothie to work, it won't last long unless you keep it cool. Packing it in an insulated container or putting it in a lunch cooler with ice packs is ideal. Insulated water bottles are especially helpful if you're going to be on the road. Of course, never leave your smoothie in a hot car. And one word of caution when traveling with a smoothie: Always shake the container before opening it. Separation often occurs in the smoothie, and all that glorious fiber will float to the top and form a natural stopper. When you go for that first sip, you risk a sudden dump of smoothie down your front, which I can tell you from first-hand experience is less than fun.

Juicing vs. Blending

If you've ever juiced your own fruits and vegetables, you might be wondering why you'd want to make a smoothie instead. Juicing enthusiasts will tell you there's nothing like the health and energy they get from juicing, and they're right. It's an intense way to get a boost of nutrients; but even if you juice, you can still add smoothies to your diet. In fact, that's just what many juicers do. That's because smoothies have benefits you can't get from juicing alone.

What I love about smoothies is that it uses the whole fruit, the whole green. There are no leftovers, aside from maybe a tough stem on a kale leaf or a pit removed from a peach. Otherwise, everything is tossed in, liquefied, and consumed. With juicing, there's a lot of stuff left over. The juice is extracted and all the pulp and fiber is tossed (or composted if you're a mindful juicer). When you make a smoothie from the whole fruit and all the greens, you're also consuming all the healthy fiber from the plant. I find the smoothies very filling and satisfying due to the extra bulk of the drink.

Also, not everyone can afford juicing. It takes a lot of carrots to get a small glass of carrot juice. For many people, this just isn't an option that will fit into their budgets, whereas making smoothies is quite economical. And since smoothies oxidize much slower than juice, they can be kept for longer, meaning less waste if you don't get to your drink right away.

Again, if you're a juicer and you love it, please don't give it up. Just add a smoothie or two to your daily regimen, and watch your health soar even further.

What's the Best Blender?

The only tool you'll need to get going is a blender. When I first started making green smoothies about six years ago, I only had an old Oster blender. It was fine for my occasional blending needs, but for smoothies, you've got to be able to pulverize your fruits and greens. You see, plant cells are pretty tough little buggers that like to be able to stay intact during windstorms, hail, sweltering heat, and frosty mornings. So they're made to hold together. Sure, you've got teeth and you could chew your salad really, really well while counting to 100, but unless you're a bovine, that probably doesn't sound very interesting. It would also make you a bit of an outcast at dinner parties. Throwing your produce into the average blender will mush things up, but breaking through the cell structure of the plant to release all the healthy micronutrients within won't happen unless you've got a blender with some real horsepower.

My first attempts at smoothies were a bit chunky, to say the least. Even if the texture would have been palatable to me, the nutrients weren't being released like they could have been. So I got a powerful Vitamix blender. It has a 2-horsepower motor, believe it or not, and it can just about pulverize wood, although I wouldn't advise trying that little experiment if you happen to invest in one. Things that remained a bit too chewy in the old blender were easily turned into a smooth consistency with the new Vitamix, making for not only a healthier beverage, but a more pleasant one.

I can't speak for other brands because I haven't tried them firsthand as of yet, but two others that get rave reviews are the Ninja and the Blendtec. If you decide to get a high powered blender, do your research, ask around, and take the time to get the right one for you. A good high powered blender can last for years, so you want one you'll be happy with.

If you don't have a fancy blender yet, don't despair. You can get started with the blender you have now, or even your food processor. (We'll discuss those in a minute.) Just be sure to cut your produce small before placing it in the blender. For a high powered blender, you can blend your smoothie for 30 seconds. Low powered versions should be run for at least a minute. Open up the blender (while it's off, for heaven's sake; I still can't get the mango chutney off my ceiling) and check the consistency. If it's full of floaties, put the lid back on and take it for another spin. With some patience, you can still manage to get a decent smoothie out of a lower powered blender. But I have a feeling that if you latch onto the idea of green smoothies like I think you will, a good blender isn't far off into your future. (Look at that, drinking smoothies even helps me predict the future.)

Using Your Food Processor

If you have a good food processor, you can make smoothies with it, as well. Again, this is not your best option and the results won't be the same smooth consistency, but it can be done until you're able to get a good blender.

I have the 12-cup Cuisinart food processor from the Elite collection. Not their top-of-the-line model, but it's not too shabby, either. For processing foods, I really like it. While they do include smoothie recipes and how-to's in the accompanying cookbook, I prefer to save the Cuisinart for processing a nice cabbage salad or some veggie burgers. I tried a few smoothie recipes in my processor, and it's definitely more cumbersome, but it can be done. I do recommend using at least a 12-cup processor. You'll need plenty of space to mix a smoothie. Filling a 12-cup container up only halfway takes up all the room it can when it's whizzing at mock speeds.

In order to make a smoothie in your food processor, chop the ingredients well and place them in the container with a large blade. Put the softest ingredients in first, like bananas, peaches, and mangoes. Follow those with the greens, and top with any heavier things like apples. Pulse a few times to get all the produce chopped up. Then, with the processor running, pour the water in through the food tube and cover. Allow the smoothie to blend for a good 45 seconds to a minute, then check for any chunks. Run it longer if needed.

Smoothie   Power   Recipes

Let's get started with these recipes, shall we? The smoothies are organized into five sections: Sweet Start, Refreshing, Tropical, Dessert, and Savory. After you've given a few recipes a try, don't be afraid to mix things up on your own by substituting a fruit or a green for another. Taste a bit after blending, and if something seems missing, go ahead and add it.

Also experiment with water levels. Most of my smoothie recipes call for 2 ½ cups of water, but that's because in my experience, the thicker smoothies tend to be harder to finish. If you like it thicker, though, try only 2 cups of water. For thinner, bump it up to 3 cups and see what happens. You can also use a combination of ice and water - say, 2 cups of ice and 1 cup of water - if you'd like your smoothie perfectly chilled. It's most important you enjoy every single smoothie you drink. And, of course, don't be afraid to let loose and experiment with your own recipes. You'll even begin to find your body telling you what to add, as it craves one thing or another.

As an extra treat, I've added two special recipe chapters: Fresh Soups and Salad Dressings. After discovering how it feels to be truly healthy, you'll be craving some different foods but you probably won't know where to turn. At least, that's what happened to me. I got going on all the smoothies, started craving more fresh fruits and vegetables, even salads, and didn't have a clue what to feed myself anymore. The usual stuff just wasn't cutting it. Once I latched onto a few easy raw soup recipes and fantastic salad dressings, it opened up a whole new world of food for me. I was able to whip up a simple lunch and make some tasty salads to add to dinner that the whole family would enjoy, not just me with my newfound eating habits.

For the soup and salad dressing recipes, you need only your high-powered blender or your food processor. These recipes usually take less than five minutes to prepare and can be packed easily for lunch at work or school. But they're filling enough that you'll be happy to call them dinner!

Now, let's get blending.

Sweet Start Smoothies

The easiest way for most people to start enjoying smoothies is to begin with the sweeter versions. This means using things like bananas, dates, a tablespoon or two of honey, perhaps some orange juice instead of water (this should be a temporary fix, due to its high sugar content), or the stevia extract we discussed earlier. These first recipes are great for someone who has never had a green smoothie before. Eventually, these will taste too sweet for you and you'll most likely prefer to go with more refreshing, even greener tasting drinks. But for now, let's stay sweet and delicious.

Sweetie Pie

1 banana

1 apple

1 small head of red Tango lettuce (or Romaine)

2 1/2 cups orange juice (or a mixture of orange juice and water)

Sweet Tooth Relief

1 cup cantaloupe

1 banana

3 dates, pitted

1 cup spring greens

2 1/2 cups water

Note: This one is a great starter for anyone a little hesitant about the smoothie idea. Very sweet, smooth, and delicious. Try making it with 1 cup water and 2 cups ice for a summer treat.

Smooth Operator

2 apricots, pitted

1 peach, pitted

1 banana

2 packed cups spinach

2 1/2 cups water

Deep Purple Magic

1 cup frozen blueberries

2 cups cantaloupe

2 packed cups of kale

2 1/2 cups water

Note: Almost black in color, this smoothie is full of healthy goodies. Among the benefits here, blueberries relieve eyestrain (like from computers or reading your favorite smoothie recipe books for hours at a time) and can even improve eyesight over time. Also an excellent brain food.

Pear-licious

1 pear

1 apple

2 cups orange juice

1 cup packed kale

Dandy-Purple

1 banana

1/2 cup frozen blueberries

1 cup packed dandelion greens

2 1/2 cups orange juice

Morning, Sunshine!

1 banana

1 large peeled orange

½ avocado, peeled and pitted

2 packed cups of spinach

2 ½ cups water

Hint: When using avocado in a smoothie, you can choose to blend together everything but the avocado. Add that last, then blend again. The longer the avocado is blended, the thicker the smoothie can become.

Bananaloupe

1 banana

2 cups cantaloupe

2 packed cups spinach

2 ½ cups water

Sweet Greens

1 banana

2 cups pineapple

2 packed cups mixed greens

2 ½ cups water

Sweet 'n Sour

1 banana

1 cup pineapple (with core is fine if you have a high power blender)

3 dates (pitted)

1 packed cup collard greens, stems removed

3 Tbs. lemon juice

2 ½ cups water

Creamy Dreamy

1 banana

1 cup frozen blueberries

1 ripe peach

3 large rainbow chard leaves

1 cup spinach

1" vanilla bean

2 ½ cups water

Just Peachy

2 ripe pitted peaches

1 pitted mango

1 banana

2 packed cups kale

½ tsp. cinnamon

2 ½ cups water

Hint: Experimenting by adding a dash of dried spices such as cinnamon or nutmeg can transform a smoothie from dull to something special. If you've made up a batch and find you don't care for your concoction too much, try adding a bit of dried herbs or spice.

Baby Got Bok

2 cups strawberries, fresh or frozen

1 banana

1 head baby bok choy

2 ½ cups water

Pear-fect Berry

2 pears

1 cup strawberries, fresh or frozen

2 packed cups spinach

2 ½ cups water

Cherry Oh Baby

1 cup pitted cherries

1 banana

2 packed cups spinach

2 ½ cups water

Frootie Patootie

1 cup pitted cherries

1 apple

1 banana

2 packed cups kale

½″ vanilla bean

2 ½ cups water

You Look "Radishing"

1 banana

1 cup pineapple

½ cup frozen raspberries

2 cups radish greens

2 ½ cups water

Note: Radish greens aren't spicy like radishes are. Although they can be a bit "radishy" in taste, it's a mild addition of flavor to a smoothie. I find this is an excellent way to make use of the greens from my summer garden.

Blackberry Cooler

1 cup blackberries

1 cup watermelon

1 banana

2 packed cups spinach

2 ½ cups water

Strawberry Rapini

2 cups strawberries

1 pear

1 cup rapini

½ " vanilla bean

2 ½ cups water

Apricot Sunrise

4 apricots, pitted

1 apple

1 cup strawberries, fresh or frozen

2 packed cups spinach

2 ½ cups water

The Refresher

½ avocado, pitted and peeled

1 apple

1 Tbs. lime juice

2 packed cups kale

2 ½ cups water

Berry Bomb

½ cup frozen raspberries

½ cup frozen blueberries

¼ avocado, pitted and peeled

2 packed cups Swiss chard

2 ½ cups water

Figgy-Wiggy

3 fresh figs

1 banana

1 cup frozen strawberries

2 packed cups spinach

2 ½ cups water

Fresh Morning

3 fresh figs

1 large peach, pitted

2 packed cups kale

2 ½ cups water

Get Yer Mojo Runnin'

2 peaches, pitted

1 banana

2 packed cups dandelion greens

2 ½ cups water

Mango Love

1 mango, peeled and pitted

1 peach, pitted

1 cup parsley

2 cups water

Hint: Experiment with different types of mangoes if they're available to you. The variety of flavors and textures between them is surprising.

Weed Your Garden

2 mangoes, peeled and pitted

1 packed cups edible weeds (such as lambs quarters, stinging nettles, cleavers, etc.)

2 cups water

Persimmon Passion

2 persimmons

1 banana

2 packed cups spinach

2 ½ cups water

Orchard in a Glass

2 persimmons

1 apple

1 pear

2 packed cups kale

2 ½ cups water

Mellow Guava

½ cup guava, seeds removed

2 peaches

2 packed cups spinach

2 ½ cups water

End of the Rainbow

1 large nectarine

2 cups cantaloupe

2 packed cups rainbow chard

2 ½ cups water

Plum Crazy

2 pitted plums

1 mango, pitted and peeled

2 packed cups rainbow chard

2 ½ cups water

Green Grass of Home

1 banana

¼ cup wheatgrass

2 pitted peaches

1 packed cup kale

2 ½ cups water

Note: Wheatgrass is pretty sweet stuff. It also needs to be blended very well as it's rather fibrous. So test a bit before pouring it into glasses. If it's still kind of chewy, give it another round in the blender.

Blueberry Power

1 banana

1 cup frozen blueberries

2 packed cups kale

2 ½ cups water

Refreshing Smoothies

I like a sweeter smoothie in the morning, but by late morning or early afternoon, I'm often ready for something more refreshing. These recipes will also help make the transition away from sweeter smoothies very pleasant indeed.

Peachy Melon Cooler

1 ½ cups cantaloupe, peeled and seeded

1 peach, pit removed

1 large handful dandelion greens

2 ½ cups water

Berry Blast

1 cup frozen blueberries

½ cup frozen cranberries

2 packed cups of kale

2 ½ cups water

Cowboy Cactus Punch

2 cactus leaves with the ends trimmed off, needles left on

1 apple

1 cup green grapes

1 cup water

2 cups ice

1 - 3 drops stevia extract if needed

Note: This is one of my favorites! Very refreshing, and the cactus has a wonderfully mild yet tangy flavor. Great sliced thin on salads, too.

Cranana

1 banana

1 cup frozen cranberries

2 - 3 dates

2 packed cups of Romaine lettuce

2 ½ cups water

Note: During the holiday season, I grab a couple of bags of fresh cranberries every time I grocery shop. I take them home and toss them in the freezer so I have cranberries available for smoothies. Not exactly in keeping with the ideas of seasonal eating, but I love having a little access to one of my favorite fruits when they're not to be found elsewhere. A dozen bags can just about get me to the following November, if I time things right.

Ginger Zinger

1 apple

½ lemon, peeled

1 packed cup of arugula

1 Tbs. fresh ginger

1 cup ice

2 cups water

Hint: Apples can be thrown in a high powered blender, peel, core, and all. Just remove the stem, and choose organic if you plan on including the peel.

Watermelon Dream

3 cups watermelon with seeds (but without rind)

2 packed cups kale

(No water)

Go Bananas for Cactus

1 banana

2 cactus leaves, with ends trimmed off and needles left on

1 medium peeled cucumber

2 ½ cups water

Golden Ginger

2 cups golden melon

1" piece of ginger

1 banana

2 packed cups of kale

2 ½ cups water

Green Desert

1 peeled prickly pear

1 small to medium cucumber

1 banana

2 packed cups kale

2 ½ cups water

A Berry Banana Breakfast

1 cup frozen blueberries

½ cup frozen cranberries

1 banana

2 packed cups spinach

2 ½ cups water

Mango-Berry Blast

1 mango, pitted and peeled

1 cup raspberries, fresh or frozen

2 packed cups Romaine lettuce

2 ½ cups water

Summer's Day

2 peaches

½ cup raspberries, fresh or frozen

1 cup strawberries, fresh or frozen

2 packed cups Swiss chard

2 ½ cups water

Just Peachy

2 peaches, pitted

Meat of 1 young coconut

2 packed cups spinach

1 cup coconut water

1 cup water

Hint: If you're not getting the coconut water fresh from a coconut, try it in glass bottles instead of cans. Also, make sure it's pure coconut water with no additives or sweeteners.

Cranapple Splash

½ cup cranberries, fresh or frozen

2 apples

2 packed cups spinach

2 ½ cups water

Zipline

½ cup cranberries, fresh or frozen

3 medjool dates

1 banana

2 packed cups spinach

2 ½ cups water

Berry Berry Good

½ cup blackberries

½ cup raspberries

1 banana

2 packed cups kale

2 ½ cups water

Hint: Make sure you drink your blackberry smoothies right away. Letting them sit or refrigerating them for later use can lead to an alteration in flavor. Not a bad alteration, but it definitely loses that wonderful fresh blackberry taste.

New Zealand Splash

2 peeled kiwis

1 cup frozen strawberries

1 banana

2 packed cups collard greens

2 ½ cups water

Minty Bliss

2 peeled kiwis

1 banana

4 mint leaves, fresh

2 packed cups Swiss chard

2 ½ cups water

Hint: Growing your own mint is a snap. Even I can do it! Start it from seed in a cute pot (cute pots are always best), and keep it on a sunny sill. To use it, pinch off a stem right down to a set of leaves. This will keep the plant from getting too leggy. Good if you're a girl, bad if you're a plant.

Dandy Berry

½ cup frozen cranberries

Juice from ½ lime

1 banana

1 tsp. cinnamon

2 packed cups dandelion greens

2 ½ cups water

Mauve: It's Not Just for the 80's

1 large slice watermelon, chunked

⅓ cup frozen cranberries

2 packed cups kale

1 cup water

Cider Smoothie

2 apples with peel (try to use 2 different varieties)

1 packed cup kale

½ tsp. cinnamon

1 cup water

Chai Smoothie

1 banana

1 cup pineapple

1 cup chai tea, cooled

½" fresh ginger

Picadilly Punch

1 orange, peeled

1 cup pineapple

½ bunch fresh dill

2 ½ cup water

Aloe Cooler

2 inches aloe, inside only (scrape out inside of leaves)

1 small cucumber with peel

2 bananas

Juice of ½ lemon

1 cup ice

1 cup water

Note: I've seen aloe in the grocery stores more often

these days, but if your grocer doesn't carry it, try a specialty store such as a Mexican food market. Don't assume the aloe you have growing in your house is the right kind. There are numerous species, and it's best to get some grown for food usage.

Grape-a-licious

1 cup red grapes

1 peeled orange

1 packed cup dandelion

1 packed cup spinach

2 ½ cups water

Spring Fresh

2 cups red grapes

1 banana

2 packed cups Romaine lettuce

1 handful parsley

2 ½ cups water

Strawberry Bliss

1 cup frozen strawberries

2 cups cantaloupe

2 packed cups spinach

2 ½ cups water

Summer Frost

2 cups watermelon

1 cup frozen blueberries

1 banana

2 cups kale

2 ½ cups water

Cherry Freeze

½ cup frozen cherries

1 frozen banana

1 orange, peeled

2 packed cups dandelion greens

2 ½ cups water

Hint: Don't be afraid to use dandelion greens from your garden. Just make sure they haven't been sprayed or treated in any way, and that whatever you pick is at least six feet from the side of your house to avoid runoff contamination from the roof and little bits of squirrel poop. The best place to gather dandelion greens is your vegetable garden, if you have one. Let 'em grow! They're food. (Spring greens taste best.)

Mangarine Green

1 mango, peeled and pitted

1 apple

1 tangerine, peeled

1 cup radish greens

1 cup dandelion greens

2 ½ cups water

Zippity-Smooth-Dah

1 grapefruit, peeled

2 packed cups Romaine lettuce

1 cup strawberries, fresh or frozen

1 banana

2 ½ cups water

Blue Bliss

1 cup frozen blueberries

2 packed cups spinach

2 pears

2 ½ cups water

Guava Kale Go-Juice

4 guavas, not peeled but ends removed

2 cups cantaloupe

2 packed cups of kale

2 ½ cups water

Orange You Glad

1 banana

1 peeled orange

2 packed cups kale

2 ½ cups water

Parsley Shmarsley

1 banana

1 peach

1 cup parsley

1 packed cup kale

2 ½ cups water

Hint: Parsley is a cleansing herb. It also makes you pee. A lot. My advice? Don't add parsley to a smoothie you're taking on a road trip.

Potassium Punch

2 bananas

1 peach, pitted

2 packed cups of kale

2 ½ cups water

Tropical Smoothies

Time to sail away to a tropical island! Get your sunglasses, a lounge chair, and a paper umbrella for your smoothie. Some Buffet tunes would be a nice touch, too. And don't forget to send me a postcard.

Pina Colada Blast

2 cups chopped pineapple, peeled (you don't have to core it if your blender is powerful)
½ cup flaked, shredded, or freshly chopped coconut
1 banana
2 cups water or 2 ½ cups ice

Go-Go Guava

4 guavas - not peeled. (Just cut off the tough ends.)
1 cup peeled and seeded papaya

1 banana

2 large kale leaves, stems removed

2 - 2 ½ cups water

Pineapple Mango Tango

1 mango, peeled and pitted

1 cup chopped pineapple

2 packed cups kale

2 ½ cups water

Jamaican Me Crazy

1 mango, peeled and pitted

2 packed cups Romaine lettuce

16 ounces chilled hibiscus tea, unsweetened

Tropical Georgia

1 ½ cups pineapple

2 packed cups Romaine lettuce

1 peach

2 ½ cups water

Tropical Rainbow

2 cups golden melon

1 banana

5 large leaves rainbow chard

2 ½ cups water

Tropical Daydreams

2 cups papaya, seeded and peeled

1 cup pineapple

1 banana

2 packed cups kale

2 ½ cups water

Coo-Coo for Coconuts

Meat of 1 young coconut

1 mango, pitted and peeled

1 kiwi, peeled

2 packed cups baby spinach

1 cup coconut water

1 cup water

Personal Island

Meat of 1 young coconut

1 banana

1 cup coconut water

1 cup water

2 packed cups Romaine lettuce

118

Summer Breeze

2 cups watermelon

1 cup frozen strawberries

½ cup frozen raspberries

2 packed cups spinach

2 ½ cups water

Passion for Health

3 passion fruits, inner part only

1 banana

1 peeled and seeded mango

2 packed cups spinach

2 ½ cups water

Papaya Oh My-ah

2 cups papaya, peeled and seeded

1 peeled orange

1 pear

2 packed cups spinach

2 ½ cups water

The Happy Lion

1 cup pineapple

1 peeled orange

1 cup dandelion greens

1 packed cup spinach

2 ½ cups water

Mean Green Papaya

2 cups papaya

1 packed cup of spinach

1 large handful parsley

2 ¼ cups water

Shanghai Mango

2 Ataulfo mangoes, peeled and pitted (My favorite!)

2 bananas

10 to 12 heads bok choy (Shanghai tips variety; or 4 to 5 heads baby bok choy)

2 ½ cups water

Note: This is an excellent smoothie. The texture is creamy and the flavor is wonderful. If you can manage to get the Shanghai tips, those make a delicious snack on their own. Just wash and eat. I like to dip them in Bragg's

Amino Acids, which is a great raw soy sauce alternative.

Dessert Smoothies

Having a healthy, nutrient-rich diet doesn't mean you need to deny yourself of something a little decadent from time to time. As I was putting together and trying all these smoothie recipes, I found that instead of wishing for a piece of cake or a candy bar, what I really wanted was food in its whole raw form. I thought I'd have to continue going without something lush or rich, but the biggest surprise to me was finding that desserts made from whole raw foods are oftentimes much more wonderful and satisfying than any processed, packaged dessert. Best part? Totally guilt free! The following recipes put your dessert in your glass. Since they're so good for you, no need to wait till after dinner. I often have one of these in the afternoon, about the time I used to crave unhealthy treats. I can say with all sincerity that I now enjoy these more than their junk food alternatives.

Poached Pear

1 pear

½" vanilla bean

¼ tsp. pumpkin pie spice

5 Romaine lettuce leaves

1 ½ cup water

Fruity-Pie

½" vanilla bean

1 peeled Clementine or tangerine

1 peach, pitted

1 banana

2 packed cups spinach

A dash or two of pumpkin pie spice

2 ½ cups water

The Chocolate Tiger

1 frozen banana

2 peeled clementines (or 1 large orange)

4 level Tbs. raw cacao powder

¼ tsp. cinnamon

¼ tsp. dried ginger

¼ tsp. cardamom

2 cups water

1 cup ice

Mango Lassi

1 cup frozen mango chunks

1 cup almond milk (or other nut milk)

2 - 3 medjool dates

½ inch vanilla bean

½ tsp. cardamom

Note: A true Mango Lassi uses 1 cup Greek yogurt instead of nut milk, but I wanted to keep this version 100% raw vegan. Technically, nut milk isn't the best thing to put in a smoothie and neither would be yogurt, but we are talking special treat here. Don't ever get yourself all bent out of shape over an occasional ingredient or food item. It's best to bend rules every now and then if it keeps you happy and on track.

Smoothie Popsicles

2 bananas

2 cups frozen berries

2 packed cups spinach

1 cup water

Freeze mixture in Popsicle molds.

Hint: You can make Popsicles out of any of your favorite

smoothie blends. Adding an extra banana, as in this recipe, gives you a full creamy texture.

Pumpkin Pie Smoothie

2 cups raw cubed pumpkin, soaked overnight in water and 1 Tbs. lemon

1 tsp. cinnamon or pumpkin pie spice

½ tsp. nutmeg

1 frozen banana

2 packed cups spinach

2 cups almond milk

Chocolate Covered Cherry

1 cup black cherries, pitted

1 banana

2 - 3 Tbs. raw cacao powder

½" vanilla bean

2 packed cups spinach

2 ½ cups water

Note: Without a doubt my favorite decadent smoothie. This one is so rich you'll swear it came out of a heart shaped box.

Coconut Bon Bon

Meat and water from young coconut

1/4 cup raw cacao nibs

1 banana

2 ½ cups water

Stevia to taste if preferred

Savory Smoothies

My husband actually prefers a savory smoothie to a sweet one. Think tomato juice, vegetable juice blends, a salty Bloody Mary without the hangover. These are some of our favorites. They can also be used as a base for raw soups. Try adding some grated carrot, chopped cucumber, or other veggies to bring in some texture for a chunky soup.

Glad I had it

2 Roma tomatoes

½ medium cucumber

1 handful parsley

2 packed cups spinach

1 Tbs. lemon juice

2 ½ cups water

Glad to have it Again

2 Roma tomatoes

½ medium cucumbers

1 handful arugula leaves

2 packed cups spinach

1 Tbs. lemon juice

½ - 1 tsp Bragg's Amino Acids

2 ½ cups water

Vegetable Jungle

4 Campari tomatoes

1 celery stalk

2 large collard green leaves without stalks

1 packed cup spinach

Juice of ½ small lemon

2 ½ cups water

Detox Me, Baby!

1 banana

1 apple

1 peeled lime

¼ cup parsley

¼ cup cilantro

2 packed cups Romaine lettuce

2 ½ cups water

Hint: Cilantro is an expert at removing heavy metals from your system, even lead and mercury. If you or your children get vaccinated or if you're ever in contact with heavy metals, adding cilantro to your smoothies is a great way to mop some of that residue up. It cannot, however, remove heavy metal from your teen's iPod. You're stuck with that.

Cold Fist

1 medium cucumber

1 large celery rib

2 peeled garlic cloves

1 small knob of ginger (about ½ to 1 inch long)

2 packed cups kale

juice of ½ to 1 lemon

2 ½ cups water

Note: I came up with this one when my son caught a cold. He prefers the sweet stuff, but I was happy to belt some of this back to ensure I didn't get his virus. Guess what? I didn't get his virus.

Super Green Detox

1 apple

2 packed cups of spinach

1 packed cup of cilantro

2 ½ cups water

Well, Kick My Pants

4 tomatoes

4 celery stalks

1 handful parsley

dash of hot pepper (either powdered cayenne or crushed red pepper)

Anti-Vampire Juice

1 avocado, peeled and pitted

2 cloves garlic

4 stalks celery

handful of parsley

juice of 1 lemon

2 cups water

Note: After drinking this smoothie, we have never once seen a vampire. (Not even one with sparkles.)

The Fist Pump

3 tomatoes

3 stalks celery

3 collard greens

6 large Romaine leaves

5 garlic cloves

1 red bell pepper

2 ½ cups water

Jumpstart Jalapeno

4 Roma tomatoes

½" jalapeno pepper

1 clove garlic

juice of ½ lemon

2 packed cups kale

2 ½ cups water

Herbal Goodness

3 Roma tomatoes

⅛ cup dill

⅛ cup cilantro

⅛ cup basil

⅛ cup parsley

1 cup mixed greens

juice of ½ lime

2 cups water

Give Me Another

2 large tomatoes

1 Tbs. fresh dill

1 garlic clove

1 celery stalk

½ red pepper

2 packed cups kale

2 ½ cups water

Curry Smoothie

2 Roma tomatoes

1 medium cucumber

1 large celery stalk

1 tsp. curry powder (or to taste)

½" jalapeno

2 packed cups spinach

2 ½ cups water

Zucchini Zip

2 Roma tomatoes

2 medium zucchinis

½" fresh ginger

3 leaves Thai basil

⅛ cup fresh cilantro

2 celery stalks

¼ jalapeno (optional)

2 ½ cups water

Fresh Soups

After you've had the opportunity to incorporate the green smoothie into your diet for awhile, you'll be feeling much different. Higher energy levels, clearer, softer skin, weight loss and more are all experienced by green smoothie drinkers. But one other thing is bound to happen: You won't be satisfied with your former eating habits. If this sounds like you lately, then you'll love this next section. Fresh, raw soups are a wonderful way to keep the healthy feeling going throughout the day. These recipes are easy, satisfying, delicious, and uncooked!

Perhaps the idea of uncooked soup seems a bit surprising, or the thought of uncooked meals unappealing. That's what I thought, too. Then I had my first raw soup, and it changed my mind in an instant.

If you've ever made homemade soup from scratch, then

you know the amount of work that goes into it. It's hard to get flavor back into all those cooked vegetables, isn't it? Most people end up relying on things like bouillon or canned broths. But when you make soup from fresh ingredients and the ingredients stay fresh, something magical seems to happen: The flavor remains. And these recipes will take you less than five minutes, about the same as heating a can of soup!

Don't want cold soup on a cold winter's day? Me, neither. If you prefer warmed soup, you can warm any of these recipes on the stove. Just don't allow them to come to a boil. If you're feeling extra particular, use a cooking thermometer to test the warmth. Most raw foodists claim that heating your food over the temperature of 118 degrees begins to destroy the live enzymes. And under no circumstances should you microwave your raw soup. Microwaves destroy the enzymes in short order.

Once I had that first raw soup, I started experimenting with a few recipes of my own. I tinkered and tinkered until I got it right, trying to create the kinds of flavors I most enjoy. I think you'll enjoy them, too.

Each recipe below makes a large bowl of soup that's perfect for a filling lunch, or two smaller bowls great as a starter to a meal.

Santa Fe Soup

This is one of my favorite soups ever, raw or cooked. The applewood smoked sea salt makes a big difference, if you can find it. Regular salt is fine too, but that smokiness just can't be beat.

Base:

2 Roma tomatoes

1 small garlic clove, peeled

1 tsp. chili powder (or to taste)

1 small hot pepper, seeded if prefered (or a dash of cayenne powder)

¼ tsp. applewood smoked sea salt or equivalent (to taste)

1 tsp. honey

½ avocado

Blend all ingredients but the avocado in your high powered blender or food processor until smooth. Then add the avocado and blend until it reaches desired thickness. (Beware that the longer you blend the avocado, the thicker the soup can get. I've accidentally made soups with avocado that could have doubled as plaster of Paris.) Pour soup base into a bowl and add the items in the following list.

Topping:

A sprinkling of corn kernels

½ chopped small cucumber

Chopped fresh cilantro

½ small onion, finely chopped

Creamy Coconut Curry

If you enjoy curries, you'll love this rich and creamy soup. It's fantastic served chilled in the summer, and when just warmed through in the winter, it is blissfully warming.

2 handfuls baby spinach

1 large pitted date

2 tsp. coconut oil (Make sure it's very fresh and it's organic. This will make a big difference.)

1 small garlic clove

1 Tbs. curry powder

¼ tsp. crushed red pepper

¼ tsp. Himalayan sea salt

½ avocado

Blend all ingredients well except for the avocado. Add the avocado to the blender, then blend just long enough to incorporate the avocado.

Cream of Celery

1 cup roughly chopped celery

¼ cup raw cashews

1 garlic clove (Small if you don't want it very strong; use a large one for a spicy kick.)

½ tsp. sea salt

¾ cup water

About 3 Tbs. finely chopped celery (save for garnish)

Blend all ingredients but the celery for garnish. Pour into a bowl and stir in the remaining thinly sliced celery. This is excellent chilled or just warmed through on the stovetop.

Cream of Mushroom

1 pint button mushrooms (Reserve 3 or 4 to stir in later.)

¼ cup raw cashews

½ tsp. sea salt

1 small garlic clove (Or 1 large for bolder flavor.)

¼ tsp. marjoram

¼ tsp. thyme

Blend all ingredients but the reserved mushrooms. Pour into a bowl and cut remaining mushrooms into small cubes. Stir into soup. Serve cold or just warmed through on the stovetop.

½ cup water

Pea Soup in the Raw

1 cup frozen peas, thawed (Optionally, set 3 Tbs. aside for adding after blending.)

¼ cup raw cashews

¾ cup water

½ tsp. sage

¼ tsp. celery seed

¼ tsp. marjoram

¼-inch thick slice of a small onion

Applewood smoked sea salt to taste (or regular sea salt; but the smoked is worth the effort!)

Freshly ground black pepper to taste

¼ avocado

2 or 3 Tbs. finely chopped carrot

2 or 3 Tbs. finely chopped celery

2 or 3 Tbs. finely chopped onion

In a high powered blender, place all ingredients but the avocado and the finely chopped carrot, celery, and onion (and reserved peas if using). Blend well, until blender has just warmed the soup. Add the avocado and blend again, until soup is at the desired consistency; the longer you blend in the avocado, the thicker it will become. Pour soup into a bowl and stir in the rest of the contents. Adjust salt and pepper if needed. Serve still warmed through.

Salad Dressings

I used to think that salads were a restaurant's way of giving a few dieting women something to pick at while everyone else at the table got to eat food with actual flavor. Okay, I still think that way. But it's not the salad's fault. It's the restaurant's oversight. The salad rarely gets its chance to shine in a restaurant, let alone in our own homes.

Too often we fashion our own home salads after the halfhearted attempts served in restaurants. The salad then becomes a side dish at home because, while it does add a bit of greenery and crunch to the dinner table, it doesn't mean "dinner." It more than likely represents something we think needs to be there, but we'd be just as happy to do without.

So, what do I put on my own salads that converts them

from side dish to main course? I start with a variety of fresh greens topped with colorful vegetables, fruits, nuts, and seeds, which are key to making a salad interesting. But what makes them crave-worthy are the dressings. Not bottled, preserved, and heavily sugared dressings. But fresh, homemade and healthy dressings. What follows are a few raw, vegan, gluten-free dressings you can easily make in your blender or in a bowl in a matter of minutes. They can be stored in your refrigerator for a few days, the vinaigrettes much longer. In fact, they're so easy and delicious you can take them with you in a small container next time you eat out. Just tell that waiter to hold the dressing.

Caesar Salad Dressing

½ cup pine nuts

¼ cup sesame

1 Tbs. capers

2 garlic cloves

2 tsp. nutritional yeast

1 Tbs. lime or lemon juice

¼ cup olive oil

¼ cup water

Pour all ingredients into the blender and blend until smooth. Add more water if desired. Pour over chopped Romaine lettuce and blend well. Sprinkle with extra capers.

If you don't use all the salad dressing, you can store the rest in the refrigerator until needed. It will keep for about three more days. It does thicken up after sitting overnight, so you can stir or blend in a bit of water to get it back to your desired consistency.

Diane's Italian Vinaigrette

½ cup olive oil

¼ cup balsamic vinegar

Juice of ½ a small lemon

1 large minced garlic clove

½ tsp. dried winter savory (Or summer.)

½ tsp. dried oregano

¼ tsp. good quality sea salt

A few cranks of fresh ground black pepper

Place all ingredients into a glass jar with a lid. Cover well and shake before use. I like to allow it to sit at least an hour before using it, and it's even better if you wait a day. This is a good recipe to double so you have lots left over!

Serve tossed with mixed baby greens, tomatoes, onions, and chopped walnuts. I also occasionally add chopped avocado.

Poppy Seed Dressing

2 Tbs. honey

1 tsp. mustard powder

⅓ cup cider vinegar

2 Tbs. chopped onion

⅓ cup olive oil

1 ½ Tbs. poppy seeds

Spicy Garlic Salad Dressing

⅓ cup raw cashews

¼ cup olive oil

¼ cup water

2 large garlic cloves

Juice of ½ lemon

1 tsp. mustard powder

½ tsp. applewood smoked sea salt (or regular sea salt)

Spicy, zippy, full of flavor! This is great on a bed of mixed greens, tomatoes, cucumber, or whatever else you feel like tossing in there. With all that garlic, you can eat this at the onset of a cold to try and kick it out. Also with all that garlic, you can eat this at the onset of a bad date.

Green Raw Goddess

1 avocado, peeled and pitted

¼ cup raw cashews or macadamia nuts

2 Tbs. capers

1 Tbs. lemon juice

1 garlic clove

¼ cup water

Sea salt to taste

Freshly ground pepper to taste

Ranch Dressing

½ cup nut milk

¼ cup pine nuts

1 Tbs. chopped onion

1 garlic clove

3 Tbs. red wine vinegar

1 small handful fresh parsley

Sea salt and fresh ground black pepper to taste

Mustard Vinaigrette

¼ cup Dijon mustard

2 Tbs. balsamic vinegar

2 Tbs. olive oil

1 tsp. dried dill weed

1 tsp. raw honey

Serve on a bed of baby spinach leaves with tomatoes,

black olives, red onion slices, and strips of red bell pepper.

Ginger Vinaigrette

1 Tbs. white vinegar

2 Tbs. Dijon mustard

2 tsp. Bragg's Amino Acids (or a nama shoyu)

1 tsp. honey

1 garlic clove

1 Tbs. fresh ginger root

This is wonderful served on a bed of baby bok choy, in particular Shanghai tips which are small and tender. You can also add sliced fresh mushrooms and bean sprouts.

Where I am Now

At the beginning of this book, I told you how I discovered the benefits of drinking green smoothies somewhat by accident. I didn't set out to make major lifestyle changes; my only goal was writing a good quality smoothie recipe book. Instead, I've seen more changes in my physical and mental health than I would have believed possible several months back.

So now that the book is complete, what is my life like? Revolutionized. Perhaps that sounds too grandiose, but for someone who has experienced asthma as an everyday fact of life since the age of four, I'm here to tell you there are no words that can describe the sensation of breathing fully for the first time. We humans can live and thrive without sight. We can live and thrive without hearing. But we cannot live or thrive without air. I think that's what makes this change so significant for me.

I'm still learning which foods trigger my asthma and which ones seem to flip it off like a switch, but that's part of life and growing. I'm enjoying the learning process because each change, whether for the better or the worse, means I'm that much closer to the health I've longed to have.

I run now. I can't seem to stop running, and when I see the grievous and pained expressions of other runners on the road, I'm confused. I feel like grinning like the village idiot and shouting, "Look, Mom, I'm running! Whoopee!" I don't seem to notice my legs are burning until the next morning. But then I run again, anyway.

Other changes have occurred for me, as well. My energy levels are great and I'm almost able to keep up with the impossible schedule of a mom, a wife, a writer, an herbalist, a homeschool teacher, and whatever else it is I do when I'm not paying attention. I have better skin, an improved outlook, and even when I'm tired from lack of sleep, I pretty much feel like going out to do something else. (But I try not to play Martha Stewart. Eight hours of sleep for me, thank you very much.)

My diet? Totally, radically different than where it was. Through drinking green smoothies and trying to retain the incredible and healthy sensation I feel after drinking them, I cut out gluten, dairy, processed sugar, and meat. Most days my diet is about 80% raw. I realized that not only did those foods bog me down, but they'd decrease my airflow. And I'm here to tell you there's nothing I'd trade for air. Nothing. You can have the cheese and the tortillas and the steak. I'm done with them. I no longer feel compelled to eat quesadillas like they're the only food left on earth. Air is my new drug of choice.

What's the next book about? I don't know. But I'm

headed back to that woodland trail with my family, so I'm sure my husband and I will take time to discuss new book ideas. My son will no doubt be biking again. But he'll have to go faster this time. I'll be running.

Bibliography

Boutenko, Victoria. *12 Steps to Raw Foods: How to End Your Dependency on Cooked Food*. Berkeley, CA: North Atlantic Books, 2007.

Boutenko, Victoria. *Green Smoothie Revolution: The Radical Leap Towards Natural Health*. Berkeley, CA: North Atlantic Books, 2009.

Davis, Brenda, R.D. and Melina, Vesanto, M.S., R.D. *Becoming Raw: The Essential Guide to Raw Vegan Diets*. Summertown, TN: Book Publishing Company, 2010.

Fuhrman, Joel, M.D. *Eat to Live: The Revolutionary Formula for Fast and Sustained Weight Loss*. New York, NY: Little, Brown; 2003.

Fuhrman, Joel, M.D. *Disease-Proof Your Child: Feeding Kids Right*. New York, NY: St. Martin's Griffin, 2005.

Other books by Diane Kidman:

Herbs Gone Wild! Ancient Remedies Turned Loose

Beauty Gone Wild! Herbal Remedies for Gorgeous Skin & Hair

Hair Gone Wild! Recipes & Remedies for Natural Tresses

Teas for Life: 101 Herbal Teas for Greater Health

All of these bestselling titles are available in both paperback and Kindle formats.

http://www.DianeKidman.com

htttp://www.dkMommySpot.com

Twitter: dkmommy

About the Author

Diane Kidman studied herbalism with the Southwest School of Botanical Medicine and continues to study through real-life practice. Her focus is on teaching others to incorporate herbalism into their everyday lives, while living a more natural and chemical-free life. She is often found picking and ingesting all manner of weeds and leaves.

Acknowledgements

First and foremost, I have to thank my family for tasting the soups that didn't work and not making too big a fuss, for tolerating an overflowing refrigerator made up of 75% leaves, and for never once complaining that I was spending too much time typing. You're my superheros. Thanks to those who poured over this book until their eyes crossed, and for those willing to give some recipes a try. You're brave souls. And thanks to all my readers who lent their support to the project through tweets, Facebook and blog comments, and thoughtful email. I've loved getting to know you more.